The Loving Wind

by Gabe Goldman

Illustrated by

Shoshannah Brombacher

The Loving Wind

Written by Gabe Goldman
Illustrated by Shoshannah Brombacher

FIRST EDITION

ISBN 978-1-7357706-2-8
Library of Congress Control Number: 2021920222

Printed in the United States of America

To order additional copies or for more information,

please go to amazon.com or
contact the author at
primskills@yahoo.com

StreamlinePUBLISHING

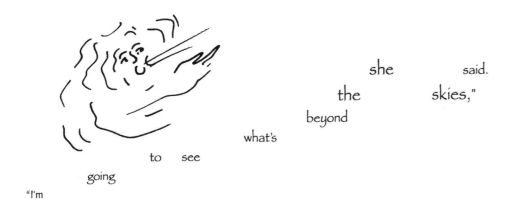

she said.

the skies,"

beyond

what's

to see

going

"I'm

I wrote The Loving Wind as a eulogy for my mother, June Goldman, who was the first Loving Wind in my life. For many years, the story helped young campers deal with their feelings of loss when a camp chicken died or their pet at home passed away. I am deeply honored that The Loving Wind was read at the stone setting of the great Jewish song writer Debbie Friedman and that the story also appears as the introduction to Sing for Joy – The Anthology of Debbie Friedman.

A Story about the People in Our Lives
Who Must Learn What's Beyond the Sky

Once upon a time,
there
was
a young breeze
that softly sang

her song of life.
She was a happy
and free wind --
happy to sing
with the birds
and free to play among the
flowers.

Once upon a time, there was a young breeze that softly sang her song of life.
She was a happy and free wind -- happy to sing with the birds and free to play among the flowers.

O-ver the years, the wind grew stronger and blew across the land. She discovered the world was a very large place. It was filled with many more trees and flowers and animals than she had dream-ed possible. She became friends with all of them.

Over the years, the wind grew stronger and blew across the land. She discovered the world was a very large place. It was filled with many more trees and flowers and animals than she had dreamed possible. She became friends with all of them.

She
o
became)
friends with the
white
pines. She became friends
with the black bears. She
became friends with the blue herons
and the pink flamingos. She knew
that color and shape made
no   difference
, when   it
came   to
mak-   ing
friends.

She became friends with the white pines. She became friends with the black bears. She became friends with the blue
herons and the pink flamingos. She knew that color and shape made no difference when it came to making friends.

Each year the wind's
song of life grew stronger.
It became so strong that it
could be heard over the
loudest waterfalls or
biggest thunderstorms.
Sometimes she was so loud
that she scared her friends,
even though she did not mean
to. She was always a
l o v i n g w i n d.

Each year the wind's song of life grew stronger. It became so strong that it could be heard over the loudest waterfalls or biggest thunderstorms. Sometimes she was so loud that she scared her friends, even though she did not mean to. She was always a loving wind.

One
day,
she looked
towards
the top
of the
sky
and said,
"I wonder
what's
beyond the
clouds
and above
the sky."

One day, she looked towards the top of the sky and said, "I wonder what's beyond the clouds and above the sky."

She asked the other winds what was beyond the sky, but they did not know. She asked the wheat in the field but they didn't know. She asked the fish in the river but they didn't know. They had never thought about it.

She asked her bluebird friends but they didn't know. She asked her vulture friends but they didn't know. She went to her eagle friends who flew the highest but they also did not know. They had never thought about what was beyond.

The day finally came when she just had to find out what was beyond the sky and moon and stars. She gathered all of her strength in an effort to blow stronger and harder than she had ever blown. She blew over the fields, and the plants asked her where she was going. "I'm going to see what's beyond the skies," she said.

The day finally came when she just had to find out what was beyond the sky and moon and stars. She gathered all of her strength in an effort to blow stronger and harder than she had ever blown. She blew over the fields, and the plants asked her where she was going. "I'm going to see what's beyond the skies," she said.

She blew through the forest, shaking the trees awake. "I've got to go now. I'm going to see what's out there," the wind said as she passed. The trees wished her success and told the water what was happening. The water told the fish and the fish swam throughout the waters of the world telling the animals. All waited quietly to see if the wind would succeed.

She blew through the forest, shaking the trees awake. "I've got to go now. I'm going to see what's out there," the wind said as she passed. The trees wished her success and told the water what was happening. The water told the fish and the fish swam throughout the waters of the world telling the animals. All waited quietly to see if the wind would succeed.

The wind circled the earth seven times,
each time blowing faster and faster. Then,
the moment arrived when she knew she had enough power.
She shot skyward so fast that her passing was unseen.
She went higher than she had ever gone. Suddenly, it happened.
She soared beyond the highest heaven and found herself---
well, no one knows exactly where the wind went. Some say she went
to a place filled with many, many colors.
Some say it was a place filled with all different kinds
of music and songs. Everyone agrees it was a place of
beauty that was the right place for
Loving Wind to be.

The wind circled the earth seven times, each time blowing faster and faster. Then, the moment arrived when she knew she had enough power. She shot skyward so fast that her passing was unseen. She went higher than she had ever gone. Suddenly, it happened. She soared beyond the highest heaven and found herself--- well, no one knows exactly where the wind went. Some say she went to a place filled with many, many colors. Some say it was a place filled with all different kinds of music and songs. Everyone agrees it was a place of beauty that was the right place for Loving Wind to be.

When the plants and animals awoke the next day,
they could feel that their friend was not there.
She had done it!
She had soared beyond the heavens
and they were very happy for her even though they missed her.
They became silent for a moment
and in the silence they realized
they were hearing a soft song –
the same song Loving Wind used to sing.

But the song was not coming from her.

When the plants and animals awoke the next day, they could feel that their friend was not there. She had done it! She had soared beyond the heavens and they were very happy for her even though they missed her. They became silent for a moment and in the silence they realized they were hearing a soft song – the same song Loving Wind used to sing. But the song was not coming from her.

They listened very carefully
and heard
the song coming from
all around them.
It was coming from the air and water.
It was coming from the flowers and vegetables.
It was coming from cats and dogs
and frogs and rabbits,
from young willows and mighty oaks.

The SONG was coming from them.

They listened very carefully and heard the song coming from all around them. It was coming from the air and water. It was coming from the flowers and vegetables. It was coming from cats and dogs and frogs and rabbits, from young willows and mighty oaks.

The SONG was coming from them.

About the Author

Dr. Gabe Goldman has been a Jewish educator for over 50 years – combining a doctoral degree in Education, Yeshivah studies, and an ardent interest in indigenous, wilderness living skills. Gabe is nationally recognized as having spearheaded the Jewish outdoor education movement in this country and abroad. In recent years his passion has been to design natural playgrounds offering children opportunities for creativity, positive social interaction, and a love of the outdoors. Gabe and his wife Pam have been married for 45 years and are blessed with four children and seven grandchildren. They currently reside in Lakewood, Ohio, when they are not camping by a river. Gabe loves to hear from his readers—email him at primskills@yahoo.com.

About the Illustrator

Dr. Shoshannah Brombacher is an internationally recognized author, visual artist, and maggidah (ordained Jewish preacher, story teller and spiritual guide). Shoshannah holds a PhD in Jewish Studies and medieval Hebrew poetry and teaches in Europe and the U.S. She lives and has her studio in Berlin. Shoshannah's favorite subject is Chassidism and her art is often described as magical. Shoshannah is the author, co-author, and illustrator of numerous books and has just published a fable about the pandemic called "The Cat in the Cap and the Better World." Shoshannah and her husband Avrom Miller are blessed with two children and three grandchildren. Learn more about her art at shoshbm@gmail.com or message her on Facebook.

The Loving Wind